# AAT

## Business Tax
(Finance Act 2020)

### For assessments from
### 1 January 2021 to 31 January 2022

Pocket notes

These Pocket Notes support study for the following AAT qualifications:
AAT Professional Diploma in Accounting - Level 4
AAT Level 4 Diploma in Business Skills
AAT Professional Diploma in Accounting at SCQF - Level 8

## British library cataloguing-in-publication data

A catalogue record for this book is available from the British Library.

Published by:
Kaplan Publishing UK
Unit 2 The Business Centre
Molly Millars Lane
Wokingham
Berkshire
RG41 2QZ

ISBN 978-1-78740-828-9

© Kaplan Financial Limited, 2020

Printed and bound in Great Britain.

# CONTENTS

KAPLAN PUBLISHIN

## Preface

These notes contain the key points you need to know for the assessment, presented in a unique visual way that makes revision easy and effective.

Written by experienced lecturers and authors, these pocket notes break down content into manageable chunks to maximise your concentration.

Quality and accuracy are of the utmost importance to us so if you spot an error in any of our products, please send an email to mykaplanreporting@kaplan.com with full details, or follow the link to the feedback form in MyKaplan.

Our Quality Co-ordinator will work with our technical team to verify the error and take action to ensure it is corrected in future editions.

# A guide to the assessment

- AAT Business Tax reference material.
- The keys to success in AAT Business Tax.

## The assessment

BSTX is the business taxation unit studied on the Professional Diploma in Accounting qualification.

Business Tax is assessed by means of a computer based assessment. The CBA will last for 2 hours and consist of 11 tasks. It is marked with a mixture of computer and human marking.

In any one assessment, students may not be assessed on all content, or on the full depth or breadth of a piece of content. The content assessed may change over time to ensure validity of assessment, but all assessment criteria will be tested over time.

## Learning outcomes and weighting

| | | |
|---|---|---|
| 1. | Complete tax returns for sole traders and partnerships and prepare supporting tax computations | 29% |
| 2. | Complete tax returns for limited companies and prepare supporting tax computations | 19% |
| 3. | Provide advice on the UK's tax regime and its impact on sole traders, partnerships and limited companies | 15% |
| 4. | Advise business clients on tax reliefs, and their responsibilities and their agent's responsibilities in reporting taxation to HMRC | 19% |
| 5. | Prepare tax computations for the sale of capital assets | 18% |
| Total | | 100% |

## Pass mark

To pass a unit assessment, students need to achieve a mark of 70% or more.

This unit is one of the five optional units of which two must be completed.

This unit contributes 10% of the total amount required for the Professional Diploma in Accounting qualification.

## Format of objective questions

The standard task formats that will be used for any computer based assessment are as follows:

- True or False (tick boxes).
- Multiple choice, with anything from three to six options available.
- Gap fill, using either words or numbers.
- Pick lists, or drop down options.
- Drag and drop, which can only be used if the question and the possible answers can fit on one screen.
- Hybrids, a mixture of the above.

## AAT Business Tax reference material

In your assessment a large amount of reference material can be accessed by clicking on the appropriate link on the right hand side of the screen.

It is essential that you are familiar with this material provided, as it will save you having to memorise a large amount of information.

The reference material is included throughout the Kaplan study text. It can also be downloaded from the AAT website.

## The keys to success in AAT Business Tax

- Attempt all of the tasks in the assessment.
- Learn the computational pro formas. This will enable you to adopt a structured approach to a question.
- Practise questions to improve your ability to apply the techniques and perform the calculations.

# 1

## Types of business entity

- Company.
- Sole trader.
- Partnership.
- Tax legislation.
- Tax planning, avoidance and evasion.

## Company

A company is a legal entity, separate from its owners and managers.

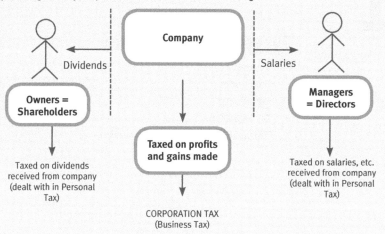

**Note:** In a lot of cases the shareholders and directors are the same people. However, this will have no effect on the Business Tax assessment.

## Sole trader

An individual setting up an unincorporated business (i.e. not a company) on his/her own is known as a sole trader.

A sole trader is not a separate legal entity.

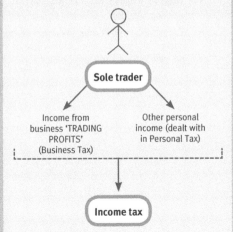

### CBA focus

In the Business Tax assessment, you are not required to complete a full income tax computation/income tax return. You are only required to deal with the business aspects.

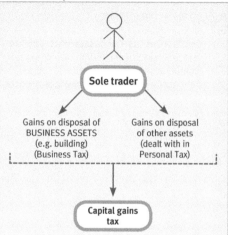

**Sole trader**

Gains on disposal of
BUSINESS ASSETS
(e.g. building)
(Business Tax)

Gains on disposal
of other assets
(dealt with in
Personal Tax)

**Capital gains
tax**

**CBA focus**

In the Business Tax assessment, you may
be required to complete a capital gains tax
computation. However, the sole trader will
only have disposed of business assets.

## Partnership

- A number of individuals carrying on a
  business together with a view of profit.

- Another form of unincorporated business,
  not a separate legal entity.

- Treat as a collection of sole traders
  working together.

- Each partner pays their own income tax
  and capital gains tax on their share of the
  partnership's profits and gains.

## Tax legislation

- Statute law passed by Parliament.
- Judges interpret statute and create a body of case law.
- HM Revenue and Customs (HMRC) administer taxation.

## Tax planning, avoidance and evasion

- Tax planning – legitimate use of reliefs and allowances to minimise tax.
- Tax avoidance – minimising tax legally, but not following the intent of the law.
- Tax evasion – using illegal methods to reduce tax e.g. concealing income.

# 2

## Corporation tax – principles and adjusted profits

- Principles of corporation tax.
- Accounting periods (APs).
- Pro forma – corporation tax computation.
- Pro forma – adjusted trading profits.
- Disallowable expenditure.
- Disallowable expenditure – examples.
- Income included in accounts but not taxable as trading income.

It is likely that in your assessment there will be several tasks covering the taxation of companies.

# Principles of corporation tax

## Corporation tax is:

**Paid by:**

- companies (i.e. Ltd, plc)

**For:**

- an 'accounting period' (AP)

## Accounting Period (APs)

- An AP for corporation tax purposes is usually the company's period of account (i.e. the period for which the company draws up its accounts).
- An AP cannot exceed 12 months.
- If a period of account exceeds 12 months, the period is split into 2 APs:
  - The first 12 months, and
  - A separate AP for the balance (will be a short AP).

### Key Point

An AP can be any length up to 12 months but can never exceed 12 months.

## Pro forma – corporation tax computation

Company name
Corporation tax computation for the accounting period ended ...

|  | £ |
|---|---|
| Trading profit | X |
| Non-trade interest | X |
| Property income | X |
| Chargeable gains | X |
| Total profits | X |
| Less: Qualifying charitable donations | (X) |
| Taxable total profits | X |
| Corporation tax liability | X |

**CBA focus**

Corporation tax is a key assessment topic. The Business Tax reference material provided in the assessment includes this pro forma.

## Pro forma – adjusted trading profits

The first stage of preparing a corporation tax computation is the calculation of adjusted trading profits.

**Adjustment of profits calculation**

|  | £ |
|---|---|
| Net profit as per the accounts | X |
| Add: Disallowable expenditure | X |
|  | X |
| Less: Income included in accounts but not taxable as trading profit | (X) |
| Adjusted trading profit | X |
| Less: Plant & machinery capital allowances (Chapter 3) | (X) |
| Adjusted trading profit | X |

**CBA focus**

Adjustment of the profits is an important assessment area. The Business Tax reference material provided in the assessment contains a pro forma.

**Key Point**

## Disallowable expenditure

Disallowable expenditure is added back to the net profit per the accounts.

**General rule**

Expenditure will be an allowable deduction from trading profits if it has been incurred 'wholly and exclusively' for the purposes of the trade.

## Disallowable expenditure – examples

| Disallowable | Allowable |
|---|---|
| **Capital expenditure** | |
| Depreciation Profit/Loss on sale of assets Improvements | Repairs |
| **Legal fees** | |
| If relate to capital item (e.g. purchase of a building) Exceptions: <br>• costs of renewing short lease (≤ 50 years) <br>• costs of defending title to an asset <br>• costs of registering a patent | If relate to revenue item (e.g. collection of trade debts, drawing up contracts of employment) |

### CBA focus

You must be able to distinguish between capital and revenue expenditure.

| Disallowable | Allowable |
|---|---|
| **Fines/penalties** | |
| VAT penalties, fine for breaking health & safety regulations | Parking fine incurred by employee (but not directors) |
| **Donations** | |
| To political parties <br><br>Donations to national charities – deducted separately in arriving at taxable total profit | To local charities – effectively advertising |
| **Entertaining** | |
| Customers | Staff |

| Disallowable | Allowable |
|---|---|
| **Irrecoverable (impaired/bad) debts** | |
| Write off of non-trade debt | Write off of trade debt |
| | Any provision in company accounts prepared under IFRS® Standards |
| **Interest payable** | |
| Interest paid on non-trading loans (e.g. on loan to acquire investment property) | Interest paid on trading loans (e.g. bank overdraft, loan notes issued to purchase machinery) |
| **Fraud** | |
| Fraud undertaken by directors | Petty theft by non-senior employees |

### Car leasing costs

Part of leasing/hire charge is disallowed where $CO_2$ emissions exceed 110g/km.

Disallowed amount = (15% x Hire charge).

### Gifts to customers

Only allowable if:

- incorporates conspicuous advertisement for the business, and
- total cost per donee is ≤ £50 per annum, and
- does not consist of food, drink, tobacco or vouchers.

### Gifts to staff – allowable.

### Dividends paid

Not allowable – paid out of after tax profits.

### Pre-trading expenditure

- Expenditure in seven years before trade commenced.
- Treat as incurred in first AP.
- Allowable if would normally be allowed once trading commenced.

### Patent royalties

- Gross amount taxable/deductible on an **accruals basis** as part of trade profits.
- Patent royalties paid to/received from an **individual** (not from another company) are paid/received net of 20% tax.
- Gross income/expenditure = (royalty paid/received x 100/80).

### Interest paid on trading loans

- Gross amount of trading interest payable (**accruals basis**) is deductible from trading profits.
- Interest paid to an **individual** (not to another company) is paid net of 20% tax.
- Gross interest = (interest paid x 100/80).

## Income included in accounts but not taxable as trading income

Deduct income that is taxed in another way or is not taxable:

Rental income (Property income)

Dividend income (not taxable) — **Income not taxable as trading income** — Bank interest (non-trade interest)

Capital profits on sale of non-current assets (chargeable gains)

**Key Point**

The income is **deducted** from the net profit per the accounts.

# 3

## Corporation tax – capital allowances

- Introduction.
- Plant and machinery – qualifying expenditure.
- Pro forma – capital allowances.
- Plant and machinery – the allowances.
- Capital allowances computation.
- Short Life Assets.
- Business cessation.
- Approach to computational questions.

## CBA focus

Capital allowances are a very important topic for assessment purposes. Tasks can involve a company or an unincorporated business.

## Introduction

- Depreciation is disallowable for tax purposes.
- Tax relief for capital expenditure is given through capital allowances.
- But note that capital allowances are only available on certain types of expenditure (i.e. plant and machinery).
- Capital allowances are:
  - Calculated for a company's accounting period
  - Deducted from adjusted trading profits.

## Plant and machinery – qualifying expenditure

'Plant' is an item **with which** the trade is carried on (active function) and not the setting **in which** it is carried on (passive function).

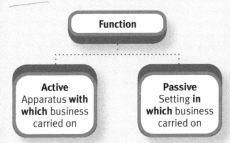

**Function**

**Active**
Apparatus **with which** business carried on

**Passive**
Setting **in which** business carried on

The most common types of expenditure that you will find in an assessment question that qualify for capital allowances as 'plant and machinery' are:

- Plant, machinery or equipment
- Fixtures and fittings
- Motor vehicles including cars, vans and lorries
- Computer equipment and software.

### Key Point

Vans and lorries are treated like plant and machinery and not like motor cars.

## Pro forma – capital allowances

| | AIA/FYA | General pool | Special rate pool | Short life asset | Allowances |
|---|---|---|---|---|---|
| | £ | £ | £ | £ | £ |
| TWDV b/f | | X | X | X | |
| Additions: | | | | | |
| Not qualifying for AIA or FYA: | | | | | |
| Cars (51-110g/km) | | X | | | |
| Cars (over 110g/km) | | | X | | |
| Qualifying for AIA: | | | | | |
| Plant and machinery | X | | | | |
| AIA (do not exceed maximum) | (X) | | | | X |
| Transfer to general pool | | X | | | |
| Disposals (lower of original cost and sale proceeds) | | (X) | (X) | (X) | |
| | | X | X | X | |
| BA/ (BC) | | | | X/ (X) | X/ (X) |
| | | | | Nil | |
| Small pools WDA | | (X) | | | X |
| WDA at 18%/6% (8%) | | (X) | (X) | | X |

| | AIA/FYA | General pool | Special rate pool | Short life asset | Allowances |
|---|---|---|---|---|---|
| Qualifying for FYA: | | | | | |
| Low emissions cars (up to 50g/km) | X | | | | |
| FYA at 100% | (X) | | | | X |
| | | Nil | | | |
| TWDV c/f | | X | X | | |
| Total allowances | | | | | X |

CBA focus

It is essential that you are familiar with the capital allowances pro forma in order to present your calculations in a structured manner.

The Business Tax reference material provided in the assessment contains a pro forma.

## Plant and machinery – the allowances

### Annual Investment Allowance (AIA)

- 100% allowance for first £1,000,000 (£200,000 pre 1 January 2019 and from 1 January 2021) of qualifying expenditure in each 12 month accounting period.
- Time apportion if accounting period is not 12 months
- If accounting period straddles 1 January 2021 a hybrid allowance should be used. For example, in the year ended 30 June 2021 an AIA of £600,000 (6/12 x £1,000,000 + 6/12 x £200,000).
- Available on acquisitions in the following order:
  - plant and machinery in general pool
  - short life assets.
- Not available on cars.
- Not available in accounting period in which trade ceases.
- Any unused AIA is lost.

- Expenditure in excess of AIA limit qualifies for WDA.

### Writing down allowance

- 18% on reducing balance in main pool.
- 6% on reducing balance in special rate pool (since 1/6 April 2019; 8% previously)
- Time apportion if accounting period is not 12 months.
- If accounting period straddles 1/6 April 2019 a hybrid allowance should be used. For example, in the year ended 30 June 2019 a WDA of 7.5% (9/12 x 8% + 3/12 x 6%) (round to 2d.p.).

### Small pools writing down allowance

- Applies to the main pool and special rate pool only
  - can claim on either or both pools
  - claim is optional.
- Available where the balance on the pool after current period additions and disposals is ≤ £1,000.

- WDA = any amount up to £1,000 for a 12 month period.
- Time apportion if period of account is not 12 months.

**First Year Allowance (FYAs)**

- 100% allowance in accounting period of purchase for expenditure on cars with $CO_2$ emissions of 50g/km or less.
- Never time apportioned if accounting period is not 12 months – always given in full.

**CBA focus**

The rates of capital allowances will be given to you in the assessment.

**Balancing adjustments**

- Assets disposed of:
    - Deduct the sale proceeds from the relevant pool.
    - The amount deducted can never exceed the original cost of the asset.
    - A balancing adjustment may arise.

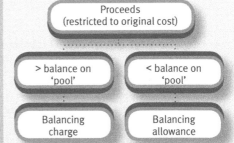

**Exception:**
A balancing allowance is never given on the general pool or special rate pool until the business ceases to trade.

## Capital allowances computation

- General pool
  - Includes most items of plant and machinery
  - WDA is calculated on the balance on the pool, not on individual assets
  - 18% WDA.
- Special rate pool
  - cars with $CO_2$ emissions exceeding 110g/km
  - 6% (8%) WDA
- Assets acquired:
  - Expenditure added to relevant pool
  - AIA for qualifying assets
  - 100% FYA for qualifying assets.

## Short Life Assets

- Each short life asset has its own pool.
- AIA available.
- Short life means < 8 years useful life.
- A balancing allowance/charge will arise when the asset is disposed of.
- Beneficial where asset with a short life is to be disposed of for a value which is less than its TWDV.
- Not beneficial if the expenditure wholly covered by the AIA.
- Not available for motor cars.
- If the asset is not disposed of within 8 years after the end of the accounting period in which it was acquired
  - the TWDV is transferred to the general pool.
- Election required for SLA treatment:
  - within 2 years of the end of the accounting period in which the asset was acquired.

You need to understand the treatment of short life assets and be able to explain it in an answer as well as be able to calculate any allowances.

## Business cessation

In the final accounting period:

- Additions and disposals are allocated to the relevant pools.
- No AIAs, WDAs or FYAs are given.
- Balancing adjustments arise on each pool to bring the TWDV down to nil:
  - TWDV positive – allowance given
  - TWDV negative – charge arises.

Business cessation is a popular topic.

## Approach to computational questions

Adopt the following step-by-step approach:

1    Read the information in the question and decide how many columns/pools you will require.

2    Draft the layout and insert the TWDV b/f (does not apply in a new trade).

3    Insert additions not eligible for the AIA or FYAs into the appropriate column.

4    Insert additions eligible for the AIA in the first column, then allocate the AIA to the additions, in the appropriate order.

5    Deal with any disposal by deducting the lower of cost and sale proceeds.

6    Calculate the WDA at the appropriate rate on each of the pools.
     Remember to watch for short periods.

7    Insert additions qualifying for 100% FYA in the first column and give 100% FYA.

8    Calculate the TWDV to carry forward to the next accounting period and add the 'total allowances' column.

9    Deduct the total allowances from the tax adjusted trading profits if required.

# 4

## Corporation tax – computation of liability

- Taxable total profits.
- Long periods of account.
- Corporation tax liability.

### CBA focus

The calculation of a company's taxable total profits is very likely to be tested in your assessment.

### CBA focus

Use the following pro forma to help you adopt a methodical approach in computing a company's taxable profits.

Note that the Business Tax reference material provided in your assessment contains a pro forma.

## Taxable total profits

Company name
Corporation tax computation for the XX months ended .......

|  | £ |
|---|---|
| Trading profits (Chapters 2 & 3) | X |
| Non-trade interest | X |
| Property income | X |
| Chargeable gains | X |
| Total profits | X |
| Less: Qualifying charitable donations | (X) |
| Taxable total profits | X |

## Non-trade interest

- All interest receivable less interest payable on loans used for non-trading purposes is netted off and taxed as non-trade interest.

- In the assessment, assume that all interest receivable is for non-trade purposes (e.g. interest receivable on bank/building society accounts).

Interest payable

Non-trade loans      Trade loans

↓                ↓

Deduction from non-trade interest income

Deduction from trading profits

(e.g. loan to purchase investment property or shares in another company)

(e.g. bank overdraft interest, loan to acquire plant, machinery, factory)

### Key Point

Interest payable by a company on a loan to acquire a property which is rented out is deductible from non-trade interest income and **not property income**.

- Include the **gross** amount of interest accrued in the accounting period.

- May need to gross up interest paid to an individual (interest x 100/80).

- You never gross up interest received from or paid to a bank or another company.

## Property income – Rental income

- Property income figure will be given in the assessment.
- Calculation of property income is not assessable in the Business Tax paper.

## Chargeable gains

- Calculate capital gains/losses on individual assets disposed of (see Chapter 14).

|  | £ |
|---|---|
| Current year gains | X |
| Current year losses | (X) |
| Net gains in year | X |
| Less: Capital losses b/f | (X) |
| Net chargeable gains | X |

- Include net chargeable gains in taxable total profits.

## Qualifying charitable donations

- Qualifying charitable donations (QCDs) = all charitable donations which are not relieved as trade expenses (e.g. donations to national charities).
- These are paid gross by companies.
- Deduct amount paid (not accrued) in the accounting period.

## Long periods of account

Where a company's accounts cover a period exceeding 12 months, there are two accounting periods (AP):

- AP 1 – first 12 months
- AP 2 – the balance of the period.
- Profits are allocated to the APs as follows:

| Item | Method of allocation |
|------|---------------------|
| Adjusted trading profits before CAs | Time apportioned |
| Capital allowances (CAs) | Separate computation for each AP |
| Property income (Rents) | Period for which accrued |
| Non-trade interest | Period for which accrued |
| Chargeable capital gains | Period of disposal |
| Qualifying charitable donations | Period paid |

## Corporation tax liability

- Corporation tax is paid on the company's taxable total profits.
- For FY2020 i.e. accounting periods ending before/on 31 March 2021, there is only one rate of corporation tax, which is applied to taxable total profits.

|  | £ |
| --- | --- |
| Taxable total profits | X |
| Corporation tax liability @ 19% | X |

### Financial year (FY)

The rates of tax are fixed for a FY.

FY runs from 1 April to 31 March, and is labelled by the calendar year in which it starts, (e.g. 1 April 2020– 31 March 2021 is FY2020).

The corporation tax rate in FY2019 was also 19%.

# 5

## Corporation tax – reliefs and other tax issues

- Trading losses.
- Trading loss pro forma.
- Choice of loss relief.
- Capital losses.
- Research and development (R&D) tax credits.
- Personal service companies (IR35).
- Deemed employment charge.

## Trading losses

- A trading loss is calculated in the same way as a trading profit:

|  | £ |
|---|---|
| Adjusted trading profit/(loss) | X |
| Less: Capital allowances | (X) |
| Trading profit/(loss) | A |

- If 'A' is a loss the trading profit assessment is nil.

- The trading loss (A) can be relieved as follows:
  - Current year relief
  - Carry back relief
  - Carry forward relief.

CBA focus

Trading losses are an important topic and very likely to be assessed.

## Summary of reliefs

| Carry forward relief | Current year relief | Carry back relief |
|---|---|---|
| | | Current year offset first then carry back 12 months |
| <ul><li>Offset against<ul><li>Total profits (income and gains)</li><li>Before qualifying charitable donations (QCDs)</li></ul></li><li>Optional claim</li><li>May choose how much to offset</li></ul>All losses can be carried forward indefinitely. | <ul><li>Offset against<ul><li>Total profits (income and gains)</li><li>Before qualifying charitable donations (QCDs)</li></ul></li><li>QCD relief is lost if no profits to offset</li><li>Must offset maximum amount possible if claimed</li><li>Optional claim</li><li>Carry forward any remaining losses after current year and carry back relief have been claimed</li></ul> | |

## Trading loss pro forma

| Year ended 31 March | 2019 | 2020 | 2021 |
|---|---|---|---|
| | £ | £ | £ |
| Trading profit | X | Nil | X |
| | | | |
| Other income | X | X | X |
| Net chargeable gains | X | X | X |
| Total profits | X | X | X |
| Loss relief | | | |
| – Current year | | (X)1 | |
| – Carry back | (X)2 | | |
| – Carry forward | | | (X)3 |
| | Nil | Nil | X |
| Qualifying charitable donations | Wasted | Wasted | (X) |
| Taxable total profits | Nil | Nil | X |

2020 is the loss-making year. The trading profit assessment in this year is nil.

Keep a separate memorandum of the loss and how it is utilised.

Assuming there is sufficient loss available, and assuming that the loss is being relieved as early as possible, the order in which to offset the loss is as follows:

1   Current year relief; in the year the loss is made.

2   Prior year relief; carrying available losses for offset back 12 months.

3   Future year relief; against total profits.

### Previous AP < 12 months

- Losses can be carried back 12 months.
- If the previous AP was < 12 months then the loss can be carried back again.

e.g. if the previous AP was 9 months to 31 December 2019, then after relieving total profits of the 9 month period, the loss can be carried back and set against 3/12 of the profits for the year ended 31 March 2019.

Use the loss pro forma to help you adopt a methodical approach to a question involving trading losses. Use a loss memorandum to keep track of how the loss has been offset.

## Choice of loss relief

### Factors influencing choice of loss relief

Rate of tax.

- Save tax at the highest tax rate.

Cash flow.

- A carry back claim may result in a repayment of tax.
- A carry forward claim will only result in a reduction of future tax.

QCDs.

- A current year or carry back claim may result in wastage of QCDs.

CBA focus

You may have to make a choice of relief in the assessment and/or may be asked about what factors a company should take into account when choosing the best relief.

## Capital losses

- Automatically relieved against current year gains.
- Any excess losses are carried forward and relieved against first available future gains.

Key Point

Capital losses:

- Cannot be carried back.
- Can only be relieved against gains (i.e. not other income).

## Research and development (R&D) tax credits

- Designed to encourage investment in R&D.
- Applies to small and medium sized enterprises (SMEs).
- Allows companies to claim 230% of the cost of qualifying expenditure as an allowable expense.
- Qualifying expenditure must be revenue expenditure.
- Losses due to the R&D enhanced expenditure can be
  - Used as normal, or
  - Surrendered for a cash payment of 14.5%.

### CBA focus

The definition of an SME and the rate of relief available are provided in the reference material available in the assessment.

## **Personal service companies (IR35)**

- Legislation on personal service companies (PSCs), often called IR35, attacks tax avoidance which uses a company to disguise an employment relationship.

- Individual contracts his/her services to a client via his/her PSC which receives a fee rather than the worker receiving a salary direct.

- Avoids employee and employer NICs and deduction of tax at source through PAYE.

- Not limited to employees contracting with their former employer, but covers anything that is deemed to be a 'relevant engagement'.

- A relevant engagement is a contract between the PSC and the client which would have been a contract of employment in the absence of the PSC.

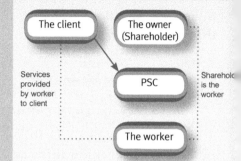

Factors indicating a relevant engagement:

- Worker is provided with tools by the client.
- Worker has to work at set hours.
- Worker cannot send a substitute.

## Deemed employment charge

The client company is not affected by the PSC legislation. It is only the PSC that is affected.

The PSC has to:

- Treat the income from relevant engagements arising in a tax year as if it were paid out as salary to the employee.

- Account for the income tax and NIC on the notional salary.

- This notional salary is deemed paid at the end of the tax year.

- Only expenses typically allowed to employees, plus a flat rate 5% deduction, can be deducted from the notional salary.

# 6

## Corporation tax – payment and administration

- Payment of corporation tax.
- Definition of a 'large' company.
- Corporation tax self-assessment.
- HMRC compliance checks.
- Appeals.
- Record keeping.

## CBA focus

Payment and administration will be tested in your assessment.

It could be the subject of a free text written question.

Note that the Business Tax reference material provided in your assessment covers most of the dates and penalty details covered in this chapter.

## Payment of corporation tax

| Payment date | |
|---|---|
| • Normal date | • 9 months and 1 day after end of AP |
| • 'Large' company (see next page) | • 4 quarterly instalments: on 14th of months 7, 10, 13 and 16 after start of AP |
| | • Based on estimated liability for the year |
| | • Payments must be reviewed and revised as necessary at each instalment date |
| Interest on unpaid tax | • Charged from due date |
| | • Include as non-trade interest paid |
| Interest received on overpaid tax | • Earned from later of due date or date tax was originally paid |
| | • Include in non-trade interest received |

CBA focus

Calculations of interest are unlikely to be tested in the CBA.

# Definition of a 'large' company

A 'large' company is one with augmented profits of more than £1,500,000.

This threshold is time apportioned for short accounting periods and may have to be divided between 51% group companies.

## Augmented profits

- Augmented profits are the company's taxable total profits plus its dividend income.
- Dividends received from 51% group companies are ignored when calculating augmented profits.

## 51% group companies

- Two companies are 51% group companies if:
  - one is a 51% subsidiary of the other, or
  - both are 51% subsidiaries of the same company.
- A 51% subsidiary is one where more than 50% of the shares are owned.

## Corporation tax self-assessment

- Company must notify HM Revenue & Customs (HMRC) when its first accounting period begins, within 3 months of the start of the accounting period.

### Corporation Tax Return Filing date

Required to file a tax return (CT600) when company receives a notice

If not received

Company must notify HMRC within 12 months of the end of the accounting period

Return must be made

Within 12 months of the end of the period or, if later, three months from the date of the notice requiring the return.
Returns must be filed online.

## Amendment of tax returns:

| By | Time limit |
|---|---|
| Company | within 12 months of the due filing date |
| HMRC | within 9 months of the actual filing date |

- Company can recover overpaid tax within 4 years of the end of the accounting period.

## Penalties for late filing

| Period of delay | Penalty |
|---|---|
| Up to 3 months | £100 |
| > 3 – 6 months late | £200 |
| 6 – 12 months late | £200 + 10% of tax due |
| > 12 months late | £200 + 20% of tax due |

## Penalties for incorrect returns

| Behaviour | Maximum penalty as % of revenue lost |
|---|---|
| Mistake | No penalty |
| Failure to take reasonable care | 30% |
| Deliberate understatement | 70% |
| Deliberate understatement with concealment | 100% |

## Failure to notify penalty

- If a company has a corporation tax liability but does not receive a 'Notice to deliver a tax return' from HMRC, then they must notify HMRC within 12 months of the AP end.
- Failure to notify will result in a penalty which is a % of the tax due.

| Type of failure | Maximum penalty as % of tax due |
|---|---|
| Non deliberate | 30% |
| Deliberate but not concealed | 70% |
| Deliberate and concealed | 100% |

## Reduction of penalties

- Penalties can be reduced for disclosure of information and for cooperation with HMRC.
- Penalties are not charged if the taxpayer has a 'reasonable excuse'. Lack of funds to pay tax is not a reasonable excuse.

## HMRC compliance checks

- HMRC must give written notice of their intention to commence a compliance check (enquiry) into a tax return.
- Time limit to make a compliance check where a return is submitted on time
  - 12 months after actual filing date.
- Where a return is submitted late the time limit is extended to:
  - 12 months after 31 January, 30 April, 31 July, or 31 October following the actual date of filing the return.
- Penalty for failure to produce documents:
  - £300 plus £60 per day if failure continues.
- A compliance check ends when HMRC gives notice.

## Appeals

- Taxpayer's appeals to resolve disputes with HMRC are to the Tax Tribunal.
- Appeals on points of law (not fact) are allowed to the Court of Appeal and the Supreme Court (formerly the House of Lords).

## Record keeping

- Company must keep records until later of:
  - 6 years from end of accounting period
  - The date an enquiry is completed
  - The date after which enquiries cannot commence.
- Penalty for not keeping records = £3,000 per accounting period affected.

# 7

# Sole traders

- Introduction.
- Badges of trade.
- Adjustment of trading profits.
- Differences from a company.
- Capital allowances.
- Trading allowance.

## CBA focus

It is important to understand the differences between the taxation of a company and an unincorporated business.

## Introduction

**Sole traders:**

- An individual who has set up a business.
- The business is not a separate legal entity.
- The individual pays tax on the income/gains of the business:
  - Income tax on income (e.g. trading profit)
  - Capital gains tax on the chargeable gains (see Chapter 16).

## Badges of trade

- Factors to consider:

| Test | Consider |
|------|----------|
| Profit seeking motive | Intention to profit from transaction indicates trading |
| Number of transactions | Repeated transactions indicate trading |
| Nature of asset | Is asset purchased for personal use, as an investment or for trading purposes? Some assets are more normally purchased for personal reasons/ investment (e.g. painting), than for trading purposes (e.g. toilet rolls) |
| Existence of similar trading transactions or interests | Transactions similar to an existing trade of the individual are more likely to indicate trading than unrelated transactions |

| Changes to the asset | Work carried out to make asset more marketable may indicate trading |
|------|----------|
| The way the sale was carried out | Forced sale to raise cash indicates not trading |
| The source of finance | Purchase of asset funded by a loan to be paid off on disposal indicates trading |
| Interval of time between purchase and sale | Brief period of ownership indicates trading |
| Method of acquisition | Asset acquired through inheritance or gift indicates not trading |

### CBA focus

Be prepared to use the badges of trade to determine whether a particular transaction would be classed as a trading activity.

Note that the Business Tax reference material provided in your assessment lists the badges of trade.

## Adjustment of trading profits

Profits per the accounts are adjusted generally in the same way as for companies (see Chapter 2).

### Adjusted profits pro forma

|  | £ |
|---|---|
| Net profit per the accounts | X |
| Add: Disallowable expenses | X |
| Income not included but taxable as trading income | X |
| Less: Income included but not taxable as trading income | (X) |
| Expenses not in accounts but allowed | (X) |
| Adjusted trading profits | X |
| Less: Capital allowances | (X) |
| Taxable trading profit | X |

## Differences from a company

### Disallowable expenditure

- Adjust for proprietor's private expenditure
- Disallow the proprietor's salary/drawings.
- Disallow general provisions e.g. general irrecoverable/bad debt reserve.
- Disallow payment of trader's own tax and NIC.

**Key Point**

Salaries/private expenses of **employees** are allowable.

### Income not included but taxable as trading income

- Most common example is goods taken by proprietor for his/her own use.
- Increase profit to reflect the profit that would have been made had the goods been sold.
- Adjustment depends on entries which have already been made in accounts:

  If cost of goods sold has been recorded
  - add profit.

  Otherwise
  - add selling price.

### Income included but not taxable as trading income

- Adjustments as for a company (e.g. income taxed in another way).

### Expenses not in accounts but allowed

- Any business expense paid for by the proprietor (e.g. business calls on a home telephone).

### Key Point

This adjustment is not relevant for a company.

## Capital allowances

- Rules the same as for companies (see Chapter 3) except for:
  - Private use assets
  - The impact of the length of the accounting period.

### Private use assets

- Each asset with private use by the owner has a separate column in the capital allowances computation.
- Capital allowances are calculated as follows:
  - Pool written down by normal AIA / WDA / FYA
  - BUT the actual allowance given is restricted to business use only.
- Cannot elect for Short Life Asset treatment.

- When an asset with private use is sold there will be a balancing charge or allowance. The actual charge or allowance is restricted to business use only.

**Key Point**

No adjustments are made for private use of assets by an employee, only the owner/proprietor.

### The impact of the length of the accounting period

- Both companies and sole traders can have accounting periods of < 12 months
  - AIA, WDA scaled down.
- Only sole traders can have an accounting period of > 12 months
  - AIA, WDA scaled up.
- If a company prepares accounts for a period > 12 months then it must be split into 2 APs and capital allowances calculated separately for each period (See Chapter 4).

**Key Point**

FYAs are always given in full regardless of the length of the accounting period.

## Trading allowance

A trading allowance of £1,000 applies for
sole traders (not partnerships).

- Trader can deduct trading allowance or
  expenses but not both.
- Applies automatically if income ≤ £1,000
  - can elect not to apply
    (e.g. if loss-making).
- Can elect to apply if income > £1,000
  - beneficial if expenses < £1,000.

# 8

## Unincorporated businesses – basis periods

- Tax year.
- Current year basis.
- New businesses – opening year rules.
- Overlap profits.
- Business ceases – closing year rules.
- Change of accounting date.

### CBA focus

There will usually be a question on basis periods in the assessment.

Note that the Business Tax reference material provided in your assessment contains the basis period rules.

## Tax year

- An individual completes a tax return for a tax year.
- A tax year runs from 6 April to the following 5 April.
- The tax year 2020/21 runs from 6 April 2020 to 5 April 2021.

## Current year basis

### General rule:

The assessable trading income for a tax year is based on the profit for the 12 month period of account ending in that tax year.

## New businesses – opening year rules

- Special rules to ensure there is an assessment for every year in which the business trades.

| Year of assessment | Basis of assessment |
|---|---|
| First tax year (tax year in which trade starts) | Profits from date of commencement to following 5 April (Actual basis) |
| Second tax year | |
| (a) The accounting period ending in the tax year is | |
|    (i)   a 12 month accounting period | That period of account |
|    (ii)   less than 12 months long | The first 12 months of trading |
|    (iii)   more than 12 months long | 12 months ending on the accounting date in the second tax year |
| (b) There is no accounting period ending in the second year | Actual profits from 6 April to 5 April |
| Third tax year | 12 months ending on accounting date in the third tax year |
| Fourth year onwards | Normal current year basis |

## Overlap profits

- When an individual starts to trade some profits can be assessed more than once.

- Overlap profits are deducted from the final assessment when an individual ceases to trade.

## Business ceases – closing year rules

- Where an individual ceases to trade, any profits not yet assessed will be taxed in the tax year in which trading ceases.

- Basis of assessment:

  - Actual profit from the end of the basis period for the previous tax year to the date of cessation.

- Overlap profits are deducted from the assessable profits in the final tax year.

 **Key Point**

Over the life of the business the total profits assessed to tax will equal the total taxable profits earned by the business.

# Change of accounting date

**Basis periods for change of accounting date**

- New date is earlier in the tax year:
  - the basis period for the tax year of change will be the **12 month period ending with the new accounting date.**
  - this will create additional overlap profits.

- New date is later in the tax year:
  - the basis period for the tax year of change will be the **period ending with the new accounting date.**
  - where this period is more than 12 months, a corresponding proportion of overlap profits are deducted from the taxable profits to reduce the number of months taxed to 12.

**Conditions for valid change of accounting date**

1. The change of accounting date must be notified to HMRC on or before 31 January following the tax year in which the change is to be made.

   E.g. if the year of change is 2020/21 then HMRC must be notified by 31 January 2022 (the latest filing date for the 2020/21 tax return).

2. The first accounts to the new accounting date must not exceed 18 months in length.

# 9

## Partnerships

- Introduction.
- Basis of assessment.
- Partners joining/leaving the partnership.
- Allocation of partnership profits.
- Changes in profit sharing arrangements.
- Partnership interest.
- Partnership changes.
- Partnership losses.

## CBA focus

There will usually be a task involving partnerships in the assessment.

There can be up to 4 partners to deal with in an assessment task.

## Introduction

Partnerships:

- A partnership is not a separate legal entity; it is a collection of individuals working in business together.
- Each partner pays tax on his/her share of the income/gains of the business:
  - Income tax on income (e.g. trading profit).
  - Capital gains tax on the chargeable gains (see Chapter 16).
- Each partner is responsible for his/her own tax liability.

## Basis of assessment

- Each partner is assessed on his/her share of the partnership profits as if he/she is a sole trader (i.e. normally current year basis).

- Capital allowances are claimed by the partnership, including those on the partners' own assets. They are deducted from the adjusted trading profits to arrive at the taxable profit in the usual way.

## Partners joining/leaving the partnership

- Where a partner joins a partnership he/she is assessed on his/her share of the partnership profits using the special opening year rules.

- Where a partner leaves a partnership he/she is assessed on his/her share of the partnership profits using the special closing year rules.

- Each partner will have his/her own overlap profits depending on when he/she joined the partnership.

 **Key Point**

When a partner joins/leaves a partnership, the special opening/closing year rules only apply to the partner joining or leaving the partnership.

## Allocation of partnership profits

- Firstly the trading profits per the partnership accounts are adjusted for tax purposes as for a sole trader (see Chapter 7).

- Secondly the tax adjusted trading profits of the partnership are allocated to the individual partners.

**General rule:**

Profits are allocated to the partners according to the profit sharing arrangements in force in the accounting period in which the profits were earned.

**Key Point**

Profit sharing arrangements may allocate salaries and/or interest on fixed capital – these are taxed as trading profits and not employment or interest income.

## Changes in profit sharing arrangements

- Where there is a change in the profit sharing arrangements during an accounting period, the accounting period is split, with a different allocation of profits in the different parts.

## Partnership interest

- Interest received by a partnership is deducted from profits in arriving at the trading income figure.

- It is then allocated between partners using their profit sharing ratio.

## Partnership changes

- Partners leaving:
  allocate profits up to the leaving date.
- Partners joining:
  allocate profits after the date of joining.

Be very careful when calculating the number of months before and after the change.

## Partnership losses

- Partnership losses are calculated and allocated between partners in the same way as profits.
- Each partner may claim loss relief under the normal rules (see Chapter 10).

# 10

## Sole traders – trading losses

- Calculation of trading loss.
- Ongoing businesses.
- Trading losses set against chargeable gains.

The assessment is likely to examine losses for a sole trader and/or a company.

The tasks are often in the form of true/false questions.

Trading losses are covered in the Business Tax reference material provided in your assessment.

## Calculation of trading loss

- A trading loss is calculated in the same way as a trading profit:

|  | £ |
|---|---|
| Net profit/(loss) per the accounts | X |
| Adjustments for tax purposes | X |
| Adjusted trading profit/(loss) | X |
| Less: Capital allowances | (X) |
| Adjusted profit/(loss) | A |

- If 'A' is a loss the trading income assessment is nil.

## Chapter 10

## Ongoing businesses

Trading losses

Relief against total income of the current and / or preceding tax year

Relief against future trading profits only

- Offset cannot be restricted
- Excess loss is carried forward

- Relieved against the first available profits from the same trade
- Loss offset cannot be restricted

## Trading losses set against chargeable gains

- Once a loss has been set against total income of the tax year, it can then be set against chargeable gains of the same tax year.
- This is an optional claim.
- Note that the reverse is not true. Capital losses can never be deducted from income.

# 11

## Sole traders – payment and administration

- Self-assessment tax return.
- Payment of income tax.
- Payment of capital gains tax.
- Interest and penalties for late paid tax.
- HMRC compliance check.
- Appeals.

Payment and administration for sole traders and/or companies will be tested in your assessment.

The Business Tax reference material provided in your assessment contains lots of useful detail on dates and penalties.

## Self-assessment tax return

### Filing dates

| Date after end of tax year | Filing method |
|---|---|
| 31 October | Paper |
| 31 January | Electronic |

- Where a notice to file a return is issued late by HMRC the taxpayer has until the later of the above dates and 3 months after the date of the notice.
- Where no notice to file a tax return is issued:
  - Taxpayer must notify HMRC of chargeable income or gains
  - By 5 October following the end of the relevant tax year.
- Failure to notify can lead to a penalty. This is calculated as for corporation tax (see Chapter 6) and is based on a % of any tax unpaid at 31 January.

- **Corrections to returns**

| By | Time limit |
|------|------------|
| Taxpayer | Within 12 months of the filing due date. |
| HMRC | Within 9 months of the actual filing date. |

- **Filing date**

  The filing date is 31 January following the end of the tax year.

- **Records**

  Business records supporting the tax return must be kept for 5 years after the filing date.

- **Penalties for incorrect returns**

  Same penalties as for corporation tax (see Chapter 6).

- **Penalties for late filing (cumulative)**

  Failure to submit a return by 31 January following a tax year will result in penalties.

| Period of delay | Penalty |
|-----------------|---------|
| Up to 3 months | £100 |
| > 3–6 months late | £10 per day (max £900) |
| 6–12 months late | 5% of tax due (min £300) |
| >12 months late | Behaviour related (min £300) |

## Payment of income tax

- Self-employed are subject to an instalment system for the payment of income tax and class 4 NIC.

- Payments on account (POA) are required as follows:

  - 31 January in the tax year (1st POA)
  - 31 July following the tax year (2nd POA)
  - 31 January following the tax year (balancing payment).

In 2020/21 the following dates are relevant:

## Payment of capital gains tax

- Payable in full on 31 January following the end of the tax year.

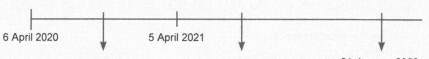

6 April 2020                5 April 2021

31 January 2021
First POA*
of income tax

* half of previous year's tax payable

31 July 2021
Second POA*
of income tax

31 January 2022
Balancing payment of income tax
- Payment of all class 2 NICs
- Payment of all capital gains tax
  (Also filing date)

- Payments on account are not required where:
  - Income tax and class 4 NICs payable by self-assessment for the previous tax year was <£1,000

  or

  - > 80% of the income tax liability for the previous tax year was met through tax deducted at source.

- POAs can be reduced if a lower tax liability than the previous year is expected. However, a penalty can be charged if a taxpayer reduces their payments on account fraudulently or negligently.

## Interest and penalties for late paid tax

| Interest | Late payment penalties | | |
|---|---|---|---|
| Charged on:<br><br>All late payments of tax | Amount outstanding after 31 January following end of tax year. | | |
| • daily rate<br>• runs from due date to date of payment | % of tax paid late | | |
| | > 30 days late<br>5% | > 6 months late<br>further 5% | > 12 months late<br>further 5% |

- Interest charged is not an allowable expense for tax purposes.

- Interest received due to over payment of tax is not taxable income.

## HMRC compliance check

- HMRC must issue a compliance check notice within:
  - 12 months of the date the return was filed with HMRC.
- Compliance check procedure:
  - Compliance check notice received
  - HMRC requests information
  - HMRC issues completion statement at the end of the checks
  - Taxpayer has 30 days to appeal against amendments made by HMRC.

## Appeals

Are to the Tax Tribunal (same as companies – see Chapter 6).

# 12

## National insurance

- Classes of National insurance contributions (NIC).
- Self-employed individuals.

## Classes of National insurance contributions (NIC)

- Different classes of NICs are paid depending on the individual's status.

**CBA focus**

In your assessment you are likely to be tested on the calculations of NICs for a sole trader or partner in a partnership.

In the Business Tax assessment you will not be tested on the calculation of class 1 employer's and class 1A NICs.

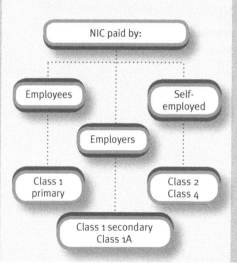

## Chapter 12

# Self-employed individuals

Self-employed

### Class 2

- Fixed at £3.05 per week where taxable trade profits exceed £6,475.
- Not payable where taxpayer is under 16 or over state pension age.
- Paid on 31 January following tax year (31 January 2022 for 2020/21).

### Class 4

- Paid on taxable trade profits less losses brought forward.
- Rate of 9% of profits which fall between £9,500 and £50,000.
- Rate of 2% on profits which exceed £50,000.
- Paid at the same time as income tax under self-assessment.
- Not payable if under 16 or over state pension age at the beginning of the tax year.

### Key Point

Self-employed individuals who have employees pay:

- Class 2 and class 4 NICs in respect of their trading profits, and
- Class 1 employer's and class 1A in respect of earnings and benefits provided to employees.
- However, class 1 and class 1A NICs are not tested in this assessment.

# 13

## Chargeable gains – introduction

- Chargeable gains.
- Tax payable.

**CBA focus**

Chargeable gains will always be tested in the assessment, for both individuals and companies. The fundamental principles set out in this chapter must, therefore, be learned.

# Chargeable gains

- A chargeable gain arises
  - when a chargeable disposal
  - is made by a chargeable person
  - of a chargeable asset.

# Tax payable

Tax paid on chargeable gains:

- Companies
  - pay corporation tax.
- Individuals
  - pay capital gains tax.

## Chapter 13

**Chargeable gains**

---

**Chargeable persons**

- individual
- company
- partners in a partnership

**Chargeable assets**

- all assets unless specifically exempt

**Chargeable disposals**

- sale
- gift
- exchange
- loss or destruction of an asset

---

**Exempt assets**

- gains – no tax
- losses – no relief
- examples
  - motor cars
  - non-wasting chattels bought & sold < £6,000
  - cash
  - wasting chattels (horses, dogs)
  - Gilt edged securities

**Exempt for individuals only**
  - loan stock/qualifying corporate bonds
  - individual's principal private residence
  - individual's shares held in an ISA

**Exempt disposals**

- sale is a trading disposal
- transfers on death
- gifts to charity

**CBA focus**

There is likely to be a question on exempt assets in the assessment.

## Chargeable gains – companies

- Introduction.
- Chargeable gains computation.
- Indexation allowance.
- Enhancement expenditure.
- Part disposals.
- Chattels.

The assessment will include several questions on chargeable gains, which may relate to companies.

## Introduction

- Chargeable gains/allowable losses for companies are calculated for each disposal for an accounting period.

**Pro forma – Chargeable gains**

| | £ |
|---|---|
| Gain (transaction 1) | X |
| Gain (transaction 2) | X |
| Loss (transaction 3) | (X) |
| Net gains in period | X |
| Less: Capital losses b/f | (X) |
| Net chargeable gains | A |

- Net chargeable gains (A) are included in the taxable total profits computation (see Chapter 4).
- Unused capital losses are carried forward and set against future capital gains.

## Chargeable gains computation

The standard pro forma is:

|  | Notes | £ |
|---|---|---|
| Gross sale proceeds | (1) | X |
| Less: Selling costs | (2) | (X) |
| Net selling price |  | X |
|  |  |  |
| Less: Allowable costs | (3) | (X) |
| Unindexed gain |  | X |
| Less : Indexation allowance |  |  |
| Cost x X.XXX |  | (X) |
| Indexed/chargeable gain |  | X |

### Notes:

(1) Use market value where transaction not at arm's length.

(2) Include legal fees, advertising costs, etc.

(3) Includes purchase price and purchase expenses (e.g. legal fees and enhancements).

## Indexation allowance

- Intended to give an allowance for inflation.
- Based on retail price index (RPI):
  IA = Cost x Indexation factor.
- Indexation factor is calculated from date of purchase to earlier of date of sale or December 2017.
- Indexation factor is rounded to three decimal places.
- IA cannot increase or create a loss.

### Key Point

Indexation factors rounded to three decimal places, or the amount of the indexation allowance, will always be provided in the assessment.

The Business Tax reference material provided in your assessment includes a pro forma for the calculation of chargeable gain.

## Enhancement expenditure

- Additional capital expenditure is an allowable cost (e.g. improvements such as building extensions).

- IA is given on the enhancement expenditure from the date that expenditure was incurred, to the earlier of sale and December 2017.

- Separate IA calculations will be required for the original cost and the enhancement expenditure.

## Part disposals

When part of an asset is sold, need to determine the cost of the part sold.

**Formula**

Cost of part of asset disposed of =

Allowable cost of whole asset $\quad \times \quad \dfrac{A}{A + B}$

A = Proceeds of part sold
B = Market value of the remaining part

**Key Point**

Cost is split on value not physical size or acreage.

# Chattels

| Definition | |  Key Point |
|---|---|---|

**Chattel:** Tangible moveable property (e.g. painting, dog, antique furniture).

**Wasting chattel:** expected life ≤ 50 years (e.g. dog).

Wasting chattels are exempt assets.

**Non-wasting chattel:** expected life > 50 years (e.g. antique furniture, painting).

- Special rules apply to non-wasting chattels:

| Cost / Sales proceeds | £6,000 or less | More than £6,000 |
|---|---|---|
| £6,000 or less | Exempt | Allowable loss based on deemed gross sale proceeds of £6,000 |
| More than £6,000 | Normal computation but gain is restricted to: 5/3 x (gross proceeds – £6,000) | Normal gain or loss computation |

# 15

## Chargeable gains – companies – shares and securities

- Introduction.
- Matching rules.
- Calculation of gains.
- The share pool.
- Bonus issues.
- Rights issues.

There is likely to be a task in your assessment that will involve the disposal of shares, although not necessarily for a company.

It is important to understand the layout of the share pool.

Note that the Business Tax reference material provided in your assessment covers the matching rules and disposals of shares.

## Introduction

Where shares of the same type in a company have been acquired through more than one purchase, rules are needed to identify which shares have been disposed of.

## Matching rules

- For companies, shares of the same type are matched as follows:
  1. Same day acquisitions.
  2. Shares acquired in the previous 9 days (FIFO basis).
  3. Acquisitions in the share pool.

- The cost is used in the standard gains pro forma as usual (see Chapter 14).

## Calculation of gains

- No IA given on same day acquisitions and purchases in the previous 9 days.

- IA is available on the share pool shares (see below).

## Chapter 15

## The share pool

Use the following pro forma for the share pool:

| | Number | Cost £ | Indexed cost £ |
|---|---|---|---|
| Purchase | X | X | X |
| Index to next event (Note) | | | X |
| Purchase | X | X | X |
| | X | X | X |
| Index to next event (Note) | | | X |
| | X | X | X |
| Sale | (X) | (X)$^{W1}$ | (X)$^{W2}$ |
| Pool carried forward | X | X | X |

**W1**

$$\frac{\text{Number of shares sold}}{\text{Number of shares in pool}} \times \text{Cost to date}$$

**W2**

$$\frac{\text{Number of shares sold}}{\text{Number of shares in pool}} \times \text{Indexed cost to date}$$

**Note:**

- Indexation is calculated every time an operative event occurs (e.g. sale, purchase, rights issue).

- Indexation is calculated up to the earlier of the next operative event or December 2017.

- In practice, the indexation factor is not rounded in the share pool. However, in the assessment the indexation factor is rounded to three decimal places and is always given in the question, therefore use the factor given.

## Bonus issues

- A bonus issue = distribution of free shares to existing shareholders based on the number of shares owned.
- On a 1:4 bonus issue a shareholder with 400 shares would receive 100 free shares.

For capital gains purposes they are treated as follows:

- The bonus shares are not treated as a separate holding of shares.
- Therefore, the number of bonus shares are included in the share pool but at Nil cost.
- No indexation allowance on the bonus issue as the shares have no cost.

## Rights issues

- A rights issue = a distribution of shares, normally at less than market value, to existing shareholders based on the number of shares owned.
- On a 1:3 rights issue at £10 per share, a shareholder with 300 shares would acquire 100 shares at a cost of £1,000.

For capital gains purposes they are treated as follows:

- The rights shares are not treated as a separate holding of shares.
- Therefore, rights shares are included in the share pool in the same way as a normal purchase
  - the number of shares are included
  - the cost is added to both the cost and indexed cost columns.
- Indexation allowance is calculated before the rights shares are added as they have a cost.

# Capital gains tax – individuals

The assessment will include several questions on chargeable gains, which may relate to individuals.

Whilst there are many similarities between the way an individual and a company are taxed on capital gains it is important to recognise the key differences, which are summarised in this chapter.

## Introduction

- The standard chargeable gain computation pro forma for a disposal by an individual is the same as for a company (see Chapter 14) except that individuals are not entitled to an indexation allowance.

- The detailed calculation of gains and losses for individuals is examined in AAT personal tax and is therefore not examined in full here in Business Tax.

## Capital gains tax

- Individuals pay capital gains tax (CGT) on their taxable gains for a tax year.

- An annual exempt amount of £12,300 for 2020/21 is deducted from the total net chargeable gains to calculate taxable gains.

- Taxable gains are taxed at 10% to the extent they fall within the individual's basic rate band, and 20% thereafter.

- The basic rate band for 2020/21 is £37,500.

## Capital losses

| Current year losses | Brought forward losses |
|---|---|
| Must be set off against current year capital gains<br><br>Offset before brought forward losses | Brought forward losses are offset after the annual exempt amount. This means that use of these will not affect the annual exempt amount. |

## Taxable gains proforma

|  | £ |
|---|---|
| Chargeable gains in the year | X |
| Less: Current year capital losses | (X) |
|  | —— |
| Net current year gains | X |
| Less: Annual exempt amount | (12,300) |
|  | —— |
|  | X |
| Less: Brought forward capital losses | (X) |
|  | —— |
| Taxable gains | X |
|  | —— |

## Transactions not at arm's length

* Use market value instead of actual proceeds.
  Note that market value then becomes the recipient's 'cost'.
* Applies to:
  – Gifts
  – Disposals to connected persons.

**Connected persons**

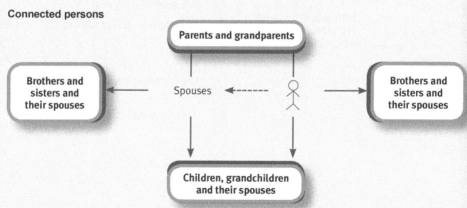

Civil partners and their relatives (as above) are also connected persons.

# Transfers between spouses/ civil partners

- Take place on a no gain/no loss basis.
- Assets pass at cost not MV.
- This treatment takes priority over the connected persons rules.
- Tax planning opportunity as assets can be moved to spouse/civil partner with unused AEA or capital losses.

## Summary of key differences

|  | Company | Individual |
|---|---|---|
| Tax paid | Corporation tax | Capital gains tax |
| Annual exempt amount | Not available | 2020/21 £12,300 |
| Indexation allowance | Available up to December 2017 | Not available |
| Capital losses brought forward | Offset in full | Offset after annual exempt amount so this is not wasted. |

## chapter 17

# Capital gains tax – individuals – shares and securities

- Introduction.
- Matching rules.
- The share pool.
- Bonus issues.
- Rights issues.

## CBA focus

The assessment is likely to include a task involving the disposal of shares, although not necessarily for an individual.

Questions involving the share pool with bonus and rights issues are common. Share matching rules are often tested.

Note that the Business Tax reference material provided in your assessment contains the share matching rules.

# Introduction

- Where shares of the same type in a company have been acquired through more than one purchase, rules are needed to identify which shares have been disposed of.

# Matching rules

- Shares of the same type are matched as follows:

    1. Same day acquisitions.
    2. Acquisitions in the 30 days after disposal.
    3. Acquisitions in share pool.

- The cost is used in the standard gains pro forma as follow:

|  | £ |
|---|---|
| Sale proceeds or market value | X |
| Less: Allowable cost | (X) |
| Chargeable gain | X |

## The share pool

- Shares acquired before the disposal are pooled together in the share pool.

Use the following pro forma for the share pool:

**Share pool**

|  | Number | Cost |
|---|---|---|
|  |  | £ |
| Purchase | X | X |
| Purchase | X | X |
|  | X | X |
| Sale | (X) | (X)$^{W1}$ |
| Pool c/f | X | X |

W1

$$\frac{\text{Number of shares sold}}{\text{Number of shares bought}} \times \text{Cost to date}$$

Note that there is no indexed cost column for individuals, as individuals are not entitled to indexation.

# Bonus issues

- A bonus issue = distribution of free shares to existing shareholders based on the number of shares owned.

- On a 1:4 bonus issue a shareholder with 400 shares would receive 100 free shares.

For capital gains purposes they are treated as follows:

- The bonus shares are not treated as a separate holding of shares.

- The shares are treated as acquired on the same day as the original shares to which they relate.

- Therefore, the number of bonus shares are included in the share pool but at Nil cost.

# Rights issues

- A rights issue = a distribution of shares, normally at less than market value, to existing shareholders based on the number of shares owned.

- On a 1:3 rights issue at £10 per share, a shareholder with 300 shares would acquire 100 shares at a cost of £1,000.

For capital gains purposes they are treated as follows:

- The rights shares are not treated as a separate holding of shares.

- The shares are treated as acquired on the same day as the original shares to which they relate.

- Therefore, rights shares are included in the share pool in the same way as a normal purchase.

# 18

## Chargeable gains – reliefs

- Introduction.
- Business asset disposal relief.
- Investors' relief.
- Rollover relief.
- Gift relief.
- Summary of reliefs.

## CBA focus

Chargeable gains reliefs are an important area and likely to be tested in your assessment.

The Business Tax reference material provided in your assessment contains some details of the reliefs available.

## Introduction

- Business asset disposal relief and investors' relief reduce tax paid on all or part of the gain arising on certain qualifying business disposals – individuals only.

- Reliefs to **defer gains** arising on disposal of business assets:

    - Rollover relief – individuals and companies.

    - Gift relief – individuals only.

# Business asset disposal relief (BADR)

- Only available to individuals.
- The first £1 million of gains on 'qualifying business disposals' taxed at 10%.
- Any gains above the £1 million limit = taxed in full at 10%/20%.
- Allowable losses and annual exempt amount should be deducted from non-qualifying gains.
- For 2020/21 disposals, the relief must be claimed by 31 January 2023.
- The £1 million limit is a lifetime limit partly used up each time a claim for relief is made.

## Qualifying business disposals

The disposal of:

- The whole or part of a business carried on by the individual either alone or in partnership.
- Assets of the individual's or partnership's trading business that has now ceased.
- Shares provided:
  - the shares are in the individual's 'personal trading company', and
  - the individual is an employee of the company (part time or full time).

An individual's 'personal trading company' is one in which the individual:

- owns at least 5% of the ordinary shares
- which carry at least 5% of the voting rights. and are entitled to at least 5% of the distributable profits and assets on winding up.

**Key Point**

The disposal of an individual business asset used for the purposes of a continuing trade does not qualify.

### Qualifying ownership period

- Must have owned asset for two years prior to the disposal.
- In the case of a disposal of the individual's or partnership's trading business that has now ceased, the business must have been owned for two years prior to cessation and the disposal must take place within three years of the cessation of trade.

## Applying the relief

1 Calculate the gains arising on the disposal of the individual assets as normal.

2 Add the individual gains arising on the disposal together.

3 Deduct capital losses and annual exempt amount from non-qualifying gains.

4 Deduct any remaining capital losses and annual exempt amount from qualifying gains.

5 Qualifying gains taxed at 10%.

6 Non qualifying gains taxed at 10%/20%.

# Investors' relief

From 2020/21 an external investor in an unlisted trading company can claim investors' relief on the disposal of qualifying shares. This relief also allows:

- Gains to be taxed at 10%

- As long as they fall within the lifetime limit of £10 million (separate limit to BADR).

Qualifying shares are:

- Newly issued

- Bought on or after 17 March 2016

- Held for 3 years.

# Rollover relief

- Available to companies and individuals.
- Allows the chargeable gain arising on the disposal of a qualifying asset to be deferred where the proceeds are reinvested in another qualifying asset.
- **Conditions:**

Disposal of and reinvestment in

within

Qualifying asset:

Qualifying time period:

- Land & buildings
- Fixed Plant & Machinery

From 12 months before to 36 months after the sale

- Goodwill (not for companies)
- Must be used in the trade

- **Effect:**
  - The gain on the old asset is 'rolled over' against the capital gains cost of the new asset.
  - No tax is payable when the old asset is sold (unless there is partial reinvestment).
  - The gain is deferred until the new asset is sold.
  - Indexation allowance (companies only) on the new asset is based on the reduced capital gains cost.
- **Partial reinvestment of proceeds:**
  - The gain which can be rolled over will be restricted.
  - A gain will arise on the disposal of the original asset being the lower of:
    - The proceeds not reinvested.
    - The chargeable gain.

# Gift relief

- Gift relief applies to gifts
  - by individuals
  - of business assets.
- Business assets:
  - Assets used in a trade by the donor or his/her personal trading company (i.e. donor holds ≥ 5% of shares)
  - Shares in:
    - an unquoted trading company
    - the donor's personal trading company.
- The gain is 'held over' against the donee's base cost of the asset.
- The donee in effect takes over the donor's gain which will be taxed when the donee disposes of the asset.

**Key Point**

The gain arising on a gift is computed by using the market value of the asset.

## Summary of reliefs

|  | For companies | For individuals |
|---|---|---|
| BADR<br>• first £1 million of gains taxed at 10% | ✗ | ✓ |
| Investors' relief<br>• first £10 million of gains on qualifying shares taxed at 10% | ✗ | ✓ |
| Rollover relief<br>• defer the gain against cost of the new asset | ✓ | ✓ |
| Gift relief<br>• defer the gain by reducing the donee's cost | ✗ | ✓ |

# 19

## Duties and responsibilities of a tax adviser

- Duties and responsibilities.
- Confidentiality.
- Money laundering.
- Tax advice.

## Duties and responsibilities

- An AAT tax adviser has duties and responsibilities to:
  - the client
  - HM Revenue & Customs
  - AAT.
- AAT's Code of Professional Ethics sets out its expectations of members (EPOS):

| Ethical approach | Adopt an ethical approach to work, employers and clients. |
| --- | --- |
| Professional duty | Acknowledge a professional duty to society as a whole. |
| Objective | Be objective. |
| Standards | Provide professional, high standards of service, conduct and performance at all times. |

## Confidentiality

- A tax adviser has an overriding duty of confidentiality towards his/her client.
- No information should be disclosed to a third party without the client's consent.
- Whilst acting in the client's best interest, the tax adviser must deal with HMRC in an open and constructive manner.
- Duty of confidentiality only overridden where there is a legal, regulatory or professional duty to disclose (e.g. where money laundering is suspected).

## Chapter 19

## Money laundering

Exchange of funds acquired through crime for funds that do not appear to be linked to crime.

Accountants should:

- check identity of prospective clients
- appoint a Money Laundering Reporting Officer (MLRO)
- report any suspected money laundering to MLRO.

## Tax advice

- In providing tax advice and preparing tax returns a tax adviser must:
    - Act in the best interests of the client.
    - Ensure services comply with the law and are carried out competently.
- Advice must not be given or associated with any communication that is believed to be false or misleading.

# Index

# W